THE WILDERNESS PARTY

L i,
in pe
by pι

A.B. Jackson was born in Glasgow in 1965 and raised in the village of Bramhall, Cheshire. After moving to Cupar in Fife he studied English Literature at the University of Edinburgh and went on to work as a library systems manager for NHS Scotland. His first book, *Fire Stations* (Anvil), won the Forward Prize for Best First Collection in 2003, and a limited edition pamphlet, *Apocrypha* (Donut Press), was published in 2011. In 2010 he won first prize in the Edwin Morgan International Poetry Competition. His second collection, *The Wilderness Party* (Bloodaxe Books, 2015), is a Poetry Book Society Recommendation. He now lives in Sheffield where he is working towards a PhD at Sheffield Hallam University.

A.B. JACKSON

The Wilderness Party

BLOODAXE BOOKS

ISBN: 978 1 78037 260 0

First published 2015 by
Bloodaxe Books Ltd,
Eastburn,
South Park,
Hexham,
Northumberland NE46 1BS.

www.bloodaxebooks.com
For further information about Bloodaxe titles
please visit our website or write to
the above address for a catalogue.

Supported using public funding by
**ARTS COUNCIL
ENGLAND**

Printed i̶n̶ 821.92 JAC £9.95 cotland, on
acid-free y certification.

for Andy Ching

ACKNOWLEDGEMENTS

Acknowledgements are due to the editors of the following publications in which some of these poems first appeared: *The Book of St Andrews* (Polygon, 2005), *Identity Parade: New British & Irish Poets* (Bloodaxe Books, 2010), *Split Screen: Poetry Inspired by Film & Television* (Red Squirrel Press, 2012), *Birdbook II: Freshwater Habitats* (Sidekick Books, 2012), *The Best British Poetry 2013* (Salt, 2013), *Poetry Review*, *Poetry London*, *The Times Literary Supplement*, *The Dark Horse*, *Magma*, *The Manhattan Review*, *Poetry International* (online), *Pen Pusher*.

Apocrypha was published as a limited edition pamphlet by Donut Press in 2011, and the Poetry Book Society Pamphlet Choice for summer 2011. Some poems have been re-written for this collection.

'Treasure Island' won first prize in the Edwin Morgan International Poetry Competition 2010.

'Acts' won third prize in the *TLS*/Foyles Poetry Competition 2007. 'A Modified Earthquake Scale' was shortlisted in the same competition.

'Foxes' won third prize in the Wigtown Poetry Competition 2006.

I am grateful to Sheffield Hallam University for a full PhD studentship; this manuscript was completed during studies between 2012 and 2015. Special thanks to the following people for creative feedback: Andy Ching, Rob A. Mackenzie, Roddy Lumsden and Ahren Warner. Thanks to David Kinloch and Strathclyde University for administering the Edwin Morgan International Poetry Competition. To all those who sailed on the *Antigua* around Svalbard in the summer of 2015, my inexpressible gratitude and love. And finally, much love to the Glasgow friends.

CONTENTS

APOCRYPHA

THE WILDERNESS PARTY

ACTS

Acts

With regard to these acts: removal of clothing,
nudity in front of females and before prayer,
the belly a heap of wheat set about with lilies,

a brood of men with bushy locks, black as raven,
the shaving of beards O daughters of Jerusalem,
exposure to extreme temperatures, hot or cold, short

shackling to an eye-bolt on the floor,
spikenard and saffron, calamus and cinnamon,
three hundred and fifty incidents of self-harm,

a garden inclosed, a spring shut up, a fountain sealed,
hoods, goggles, lap dances during interrogation,
fear of dogs, the use of dogs; the acts in question

were overseen by known government officials,
their teeth a flock of sheep, evenly shorn.

A Modified Earthquake Scale

I

Beep beep: a zebra finch
motoring between perches,
a peaceable age of entwined fish.

II

On upper floors,
delicate souls with seafood pliers
demolish crab claws.

III

A family spirit
rattles her own portrait,
scrawls moustachios on it.

IV

Parked cars rockabye with lovers.
With lamb's blood, the governor
daubs his front door.

V

As every pendulum fails
the sleepers awaken. Church bells
peal themselves.

VI

Citizens flee the bullring.
Radios play 'Begin the Beguine',
shopkeepers cave in.

VII

Architectural ornaments
crumble; the veil is rent.
A wild pitching of press tents.

VIII

Branches crack, a tower falls.
Water levels
rise like mercury in dead wells.

IX

Earth is open for business.
Crumbs on broken dishes
marauded by zebra finches.

X

The governor struggles to adapt:
a crab-claw hand,
the whispering toenails of a rat.

XI

Rail tracks grow serpentine,
cockroaches bide time.
There is cake, there is wine.

XII

Tidal meadows, ghost towns.
Communications down,
the angels elect their new thrones.

Foxes

A passion fuelled by foxes cannot last.
Vampires moan in sweet unmirrored bliss.
A skater's joy could make a pond collapse.
Fox-love is a game of hit or miss.

I throw them chicken wings, rags of beef.
Porch lights will ignite when foxes run.
Our garden is a pool of disbelief.
Vermin have their holes in kingdom come.

The synaesthete sees colour in a word;
a tune is bitter almond, orange peel.
A fox's nose is cleaner than a sword;
our kiss, like burning bibles on a wheel.

Hail, as foxes gnaw their daily bread,
the winter pavement serving as a dish.
We snuffle out our boundary marks in bed.
Speed me, Christ, another night like this.

The Godwit

Godwit, good creature,
leggy mudfrequenter,
your downward prayers

go rightly answered:
lithe worm, cold blood.
Fly true, spearhead,

in ceremonial marshlight,
lapwing and snipe
your freshwater allies.

Grim heron, merry stoat
in kung-fu shoes: threat,
your chicks' fate.

Godwit, overwintering here,
diminish, repair.

Treasure Island

I mumble the solemn oil-charm of 'Sullom Voe'.
Your face looks oddly slipshod or post-dental.
Half a mouth gone sloppy you cannot whistle. I wax

piratical: 'Touch o' the palsy?' And blimey, it's true –
Bell's Palsy, the seventh nerve paralysed, post-virus.
It sounds legendary, like Sinbad's seventh, or seven seas

crossed by fleece-mad Argonauts. They'd go bananas here:
nursery slopes of newborn lambs, the staggering
foals in May's heatwave, as though earth were unsteady.

I plunder cigarettes from Hamnavoe, veer off to mosey
on Meal Beach, consider the siblings 'blithe' and 'Blydoit',
my *Linux Bible* drowned, hallelujah, in verdigris shallows.

Fortified with builder's tea, accepting the unforeseen
facial arrangement, muscle hitch, you spurn steroids
in hope of self-healing. Heath Spotted-orchids are out;

by Kettla Ness, a nosey family of seals, their heads
our ocean pop-ups. They look to shepherd us,
by hypnosis, back to these whale-humps of green hills,

boot-swallowing blanket bogs, bedrolls of mist,
Burra's object permanence. The air is a new drug:
high on appetite, we descend like Assyrians

on cream cake, fancies, our chins hung with wolfdrool.
Your sister flies in with games of geocache,
her plastic tub of trinkets buried at Bannaminn,

coordinates posted online, finders keepers,
contents: Kinder egg, Jack of hearts, bird skull.
We pitch ourselves behind the prizewinner's eyes,

imagine the unlidding, Tupperware triumphant,
those penny giveaways transfigured, blindly adored.
Your good face grows back, at ease, tomato-bright.

Heatwave

Native on waste ground,
rosebay willowherb
has overpowered Anderston:

patchy river developments,
old red light, the derelict
bakery tower a pigeon haven.

And this, once: a fluttering
birdmouse, buzzing those weeds,
the mind momentarily

dislocated by fear's rush –
the Hummingbird Hawk-moth,
unheard-of this far north

and all wrong to begin with:
butterfly zeppelin, half
Tinkerbell half water vole.

In such wonders a new
testament or plague-tarot,
the heat sinful, inevitable.

Three Messerschmidt Heads

Franz Xaver Messerschmidt, 1736–1783

The Incapable Bassoonist

No blousy orchestra, mon frère,
no instruments of torture –
to absolute silence I commit

my second house, this dark pit.
Fools tune up, rehearse wailsong:
sawmills have better seasons.

I clip toenails and hear gunshot.
Berliners redden like beetroot,
all puff and brute persuasion.

The wind lifts, rain comes on.
My old maestro, Carlos Kleiber,
moves wheatfields in the Hereafter.

Perfection can ruin us, mon frère.
Demons occupy the air.

The Difficult Secret

Lips, what? Keep schtum,
stay buttoned. Beaked spirits
govern this mum state
with knife and cockle-spoon,

crave rosebud or bee-stung
lips, those kiss-limpets.
Airborne occult potentates
bug me, spy: a southern

pout or pucker, eyes 'molten'
or 'melting' – leaks. Be shut.
Lips indrawn I unfruit.
Should I perish, dear cousin,

follow this breadcrumb:
in forty-nine apple crates
my several heads, one secret.
Cousin, lips herald bedlam.

The Artist as He Imagined Himself Laughing

Whose laughter is broken? Which dummkopf?
Whose bellows are half-price in Hell?
Whose joy begins like a whiffling breeze
and mounts, by jaw-shivering degrees,
to burst with as much angelic decibel
as distant wind-muffled sheep's cough?

Those gulp-throat gollums, that crow
choking on whortleberries... There's me,
alive in a Slovak lambswool hat
with bowling pin teeth, lips curled back.
Whose chuckle is tin-cast for eternity.
Whose countenance frozen, whose eye-stones.

Romantic Interlude

In a moment of erotic madness
I attempt puff pastry, on a pie.
You've gone walkies. A dead chef
turns in his grave, rotisserie

chicken style. I have radical doubts,
carrots, onions, the oven a puzzle.
Come home, chuck. Tea's out.
I'm not burnt or remotely in trouble.

Easter Monday

Morningkind, we sail our Easter bed.
Moves get sprung: an Octopus, a Lovelock,
some wrestlemania before we mate,

biting our soft coin, exchanging gifts.
Shoulders pinned, I offer my sea-chains,
a billy goat also, to minister these rocks,

and fifty-seven varieties of shame.
You stroke my fur, give me your best licks,
a miracle fish made of cellophane.

Otters may astound with wickering high jinks
but we're agog as bodies dewdrop, glisten,
quicken towards O, this mounting crisis.

We lie lapwinged as dawn rises.
Long live critters in caves, in earth, in ashes.

Inexpressible Island

Antarctica, March–September 1912

Their home, the ice cave, stank.
Six men slept in reindeer bags,
three facing three, by naval rank.

Not shadows but rendered fat:
six grease-phantoms who shat
continually, their blubber diet

ruinous on morale and gut;
their dreams pudding, sledge biscuit,
soup without reindeer hair in it.

The air sooty, a black smitch:
all wept with stove blindness.
A gallon tin for officers' piss,

a gallon tin for others'. Piles,
anal bleeding. Frozen seals
chipped with rock hammers, chisels,

the hard rain of meat splinters
melting in beards and Jaeger mittens.
Cock and balls frostbitten;

a log-book, for discipline;
the rescue party of ten men,
on closer view, ten penguins.

Polar night, six months. For every ill
a Sunday hymn, a smoking ritual.
Later, they would name the isle.

Time

heals all, the armchair prophets say,
as one rainbow resolves the Flood.
So blood congeals, while memory
spins like rear wheels in mud.

Saint Brigid of Blackwaterfoot

My dear Brig, my brave daughter,
I commend your studies and applaud
your recent essay, 'The Gannetalia:
legendary herring in pseudo-Wexford

with particular reference to Kiril,
called Handsome, hooked by Harald,
etc.' Your special mind or school
is quite beyond me, however. Appalled

your mother was ... B, we flounder.
I have rumour you wear potato sacks,
clogs, experiment with gunpowder?
Eat rabbits raw? If you'd come back

we promise a new start, no curfews
or calisthenics, no 'Sleepy Stalingrad'.
The hydrangeas are out, pinks and blues.
Those conifers you love so much ... Dad.

An Enquiry Concerning Mouse Brightness

A shoebox burial in summer soil:
the mouse Mickey, pet, formerly pink
eyed, gone stiff, plain gone, Platonic,

the pure idea of Mouse, not monster mouse
or twitch augmented, no diminished
fifth or seventh or jazz funeral James

Bond style, no: a circa '73 garden willow,
shallow hole, that shoebox, a mouse
in exile, in excelsis, poor Crusoe.

The vigil was night-long, with snacks –
arise, arise you teardrop flame of blue,
you Esso blue, you gas-pilot: a soul

unhoused, un-moused, most visible, oh!
and beaming up, to *Enterprise*, amen.

The Find

1

A table top. A body object,
pocked surface hard as rock,
entirely frozen. Knock knock.

Lashes, in perfect rows,
fringe the dry watering holes;
ears are extinct volcanoes,
halloo, halloo; by one elbow

a cow-licke of orange haire.
What beast is couched here.
Mammuthus. Honey monster.

2

The herd moves. A scoured sky,
a month-old calf in river slurry
kicks unswimming, makes cry,
inhales but sand; insucks clay.

Dies then, pipsqueak; water's
lactobactilli pickle her fibres;
a truelove knot in permafrost,
a woolly morsel. Full stop.

Skip 40,000 years. Blink them.
Reindeer herders click tongues.

3

Core sample: drill this football,
this bag of tricks. The sour smell
is lactic acid, the defrosting. Small
wonder – her bones weep crystals:

vivianite, a mineral phosphate,
bomb-tick liquor, brilliant blue.
Sweat beads in bio-suits.

Stomach contents: mother's dung,
microbe rich and best medicine.
This *mamont*, this omen.

4

Satellite object, out of body:
a premolar, rough nugget,
its two-horned fool's cap of roots.

Book of *Mammoth*, tooth diary:
'Born in spring' reads dentine,
its oxygen isotopes undying

soothsayers. And here, intact,
unerupted, her milk tusks,
their seedling story of 'prosperous
even days; ending abrupt'.

'Camberwick Green'

Episode over, it's not
over. He's always there,
present and correct:

the boy-pierrot,
his clothes-peg head,
body of sponge,

in slow mechanical
motion or mouse-toil,
a workhouse gavotte:

he turns and again turns
a wooden crank handle,
that's all, a repeat

action which rolls up
a ream of credits:
voice, animation,

those responsible...
he stops at each name,
regards them, unreading,

his blank intervals.
Elsewhere, off camera,
the goodmorning Green

continues: busy bees
wriggle and share news,
the police constable

trills his usual song,
a miller grinds corn...
but here, this final

turn, this wind-up task,
and him surrounded
by antique lute,

untouchable school bell,
military drum, where
is this, The End, half

attic room, half stage;
what had he done
wrong, the child,

star of loneliness.

NATURAL HISTORY

The natural cries of all animals, even of those animals with whom we have not been acquainted, never fail to make themselves sufficiently understood; this cannot be said of language.

EDMUND BURKE, *A Philosophical Enquiry into the Origin of our Ideas of the Sublime and Beautiful* (1757)

Of Elephants

The clemancie of Elephants. How elephants
breed and how they disagree with Dragons.

How they make sport in a kind of Morrish dance.
The elephant who wrote Greeke and read musicke.

The elephant who cast a fancie and was enamoured upon
a wench in Egypt who sold nosegaies and wickerishe.

Their hornes, or properly Teeth, of which men make
images of the gods, fine combes, wanton toies.

Who march alwaies in troupes. Who snuffe and puffe.
Who the troublesome flie haunts.

Who cannot abide a rat or a mouse. Who are purified
by dashing and sprinkling themselves with water.

Who, enfeebled by sicknesse, lie upon their backes,
casting and flinging herbs up toward heaven.

Who adore and salute in their rude manner that planet,
the moone.

Of Lions

The greace of a Lion, with Oyle of Roses,
annointed on those grimm or heavie sadde,
will speedily tame grieffe. So fell, so fierce,

yet Lions will quake at Cockerill's blast
or noise of cartwheels. Likewise, it is known,
they fear an emptie charriot, fire, and Snailes.

Authorities agree, a Lion is never sicke
except for a certaine peevishness of stomacke;
the cure, tie severall she-apes on his backe:

the verie indignitie of their malapert saucinesse
may move his patience to a fit of madness,
and feasting on apes, their blood, a Lion improves.

Lions lift up a legge to pisse, as dogges doe.
Lions are appeased by Sweetes, and in this regard
resemble men besnared by foule feelinge,

be they Forresters, Faulconers, Ferret-heavers,
keepers of cattell, bee-hives, fishe-pools, ponds,
or those who licke Todes and go pigglety.

Of the Crocodile

A great and greedie devourer,
with fish-meate stuck evermore

between his teeth. A wren,
that royal bird, comes to peck,

piking, with her neb: the scrape
and scouring makes a Crocodile gape,

asleepe with pleasure.

Of Bees

Bees have a Commonwealth and regiment.
They go about in Spring, as Beanes bloume.

How cleane their hives, no trumperie or gubbins.
All filth is foot-balled smartlie out.

They take joye in the clapping of hands,
the brute call of brasen bassoons.

Their young, a knit-worke of severall flowres,
their sinews petals, handsomely composed.

Concerning honie, and its origin: a skie-sweat,
a glutinous gellie, proceeding from starres.

This substance, the aires liquor, Bees gather.
With rainebows comes a drisling dew of honie,

as lovers prove, their kisses glewie-sweet.

How creatures find Physicall remedie

On dizzy daies, the hairie Bore
recovers with crab-fish and yvie.

The Weazle takes Rue, the Torteise
drives out poyson with Marjaram.

The Storke, when bilious and awry,
will suck on Parsley.

The Snake will roil in Fennell juice
when shedding her dead-coat.

The Elephant, on swallowing Chameleons,
runs lickety-splitt for a wild Olive.

The Stag or Hind, venomous by weeds,
goes by and by to artichokes.

The Porkpen will sharpen her quilles
on amber, as will Urchins and Eggogs.

Herons clapper down on Marrish reeds,
the Raven immaculate by Lawrell.

Of Swine

Soveraigne to the games of gluttonie,
their flesh has fiftie kingdoms, talangs, tastes.

And so, the busy pen of Censor *Claudius*
concerning bellies, paps, the wombe, the stones.

The brawne, the brizen, kernels, tender-loines.
The chaw, the crisp of taile, the chewie nose.

A whole Bore at once is mightie rare,
and subject to a tax, to please *Minerva*.

Of Mice and Rats

Neither tame nor wild. Of strange token.
Sleeke, prognosticating vermine: they nibbled
silver shields and bucklers at Lavinium,
foretelling war in Persia; unlucky *Hanniball*,

after his shoe-strings were chewed asunder,
suffered mightily with shingles. And if rats
crie, or squeake in want of milk chocolat,
it marrs the ceremoniall augurie of Birds.

Rats huddel through Winter. They sleepe
in hammocks, strung between reeds, on rivers.
Their tailes allowe for terrible gymnastics;
their teethe, a mortall enemie to yron.

Their eies Myrtle berries, most blacke,
profound with mischiefe. Clawes featherish.
The principall of all rats, is play, or frisk.
They chirrup on seeing their owne familie.

APOCRYPHA

Ursula, in a garden, found
A bed of radishes.

WALLACE STEVENS, 'Cy Est Pourtraicte,
Madame Ste Ursule, et Les Unze Mille Vierges'

The German asparagus are fabulous.

GEORGE W. BUSH, 11 June 2008

I

Ruth at sunrise, grooming horses.
The bit, bridle, curry-comb of love
was *her* business.

Simeon skulked around indoors,
consulted Qabalah, threw sticks,
anything to improve sex.

Clouds were locomotive smoke,
camels or torn pillows,
the imperfect

science of moodswing or a god
in evidence everywhere, the veil
obscuring male from female.

Ruth gathered apples. The Elohim
stamped in their stalls.

II

The Apocalypse of Judas,
chapter thirteen, verse
something or other:

as cows feed on clover,
crows on earthworms,
so men desire digestive charms.

It is beauty sustains us...
lean cuts from the Cross,
Italian shoes.

Therefore avoid St Andrews,
its burnt crust of a castle,
golf ball truffles,

the West Sands
a mouth-watering prospect for the damned.

III

Bed-head Lazarus, at breakfast:
three Embassy Regal, tea so strong
you could trot a mouse on it.

To his bare barrel chest
a rag-rosette was butterfly stitched,
its filthy text: *Do Not Disturb*.

Nettle cheese omelette,
French toast with field mushrooms,
three more furious cigarettes.

Manifest ailments: eye-gum,
heart overrun with Japanese knotweed,
cock not worth a docken.

Mist burned off. Honeybees fussed
religiously, as usual, over roses.

IV

Judith spoke UNIX, cracked
other command languages,
grew marigolds in lunar grit.

Servers were christened Mary,
Mungo, and Midge; the root
passwords made fiendish.

Secure data, from cell to cell,
parleyed. Impossibles fell
open like horse chestnuts.

Lastly, for the highest heaven,
Empyrean firewall rules –
as Judith wrote, a swan's Ghost

infused her subtle wrist,
the green Kelvingrove.

V

Gasps, cries, as Giordano
unveiled his masterpiece:
a life-size model of man,

exquisite automaton. By force
of white magic or bad maths,
Hermetic mustard, this figure

sparked, blinked, spoke out:
'Imperial Chancellor, belovèd
Neopolitan pumpkin-eaters,

observe my cunning body:
composite, most economical,
powered by equinox or gas;

my feet of clay, heart of gold,
the jawbone of an ass.'

VI

Adam's jaw, at birth:
teeth upper and lower,
immaculate African

white, including incisors,
ideal for all that red meat
hoofing it through Eden.

Tales of his *wisdom* teeth,
those ingrowing
tusks of apish origin,

remain as apocrypha.
See also: Adam's puberty,
the pudding-bowl haircut,

his mother
cursing his father.

VII

Adam lay miraculous,
unconscious with drink.
In a dream, he named whiskies

by nose, palate, finish:
brine and limes, a delicate
peat-reek, Weetabix.

Plasticine, emulsion paint,
amyl nitrate. A warm horse.
Kippers, treacle toffee, grassy

with green grape...
the work was endless.
Jalapeño peppers, tobacco notes...

Adam rose with a rough tongue
and heartbroken.

VIII

Abraham wielded a watering can.
With star-mangled fervour
he sprinkled the Arctic, the Sahara.

Five years later, a riot of wild
orchids and tropical liana
convulsed the Arndale shopping centre.

Moths fled their equator.
With twelve-inch tongues uncoiled
they drilled for glacial nectar.

Some species perished: inverted
atmospheres, increased cloud cover
snuffed the jewelled frog, the grail spider.

When moonlight wobbled
Abraham knocked a nail through it.

IX

Barabbas came to Butterstone,
found his chalet, unpacked.
Self-buttered with sun lotion

he lay supine, saw June rabbits
frisk in buttercup fields,
grouse trooping through tall grass.

In Birnam Wood the Birnam Oak,
deathless on crutches,
the neighbouring Sycamore

shedding its whirligig seed,
throwing its shade. Time ticked on.
Ice cream dribbled in wafer cones.

Barabbas, in Butterstone,
saw rabbits, grouse, and buttercups.

X

High noon, Graceland:
the risen Elvis
rolls away his rhinestone,

his burger, his Vegas.
To the few, he croons,
the gold lamé

spirit upon him, heavily
sideburned in black leather
or whistling Dixie.

Gretsch guitars twang:
the End of Days
follows on that note,

our saviour a surf song,
the flooded sand.

XI

Moses horned, lantern-jawed,
down from his mountain:
the Law chiselled, half-ton,

his palms and fingertips
rosy-raw. Neighbours gawped.
Chinese whispers followed, via

fat lip or speech impediment:
avoid shellfish and homosexuals;
dally not with incontinent vipers

on Hollywood Boulevard; fear
cuckoo spit, the cuckoo wasp.
Secure the election.

Moses, in a marmalade wig,
reloaded his gun.

XII

Daniel's ear, awash with voices:
the high voltage
war council of thunderclouds,

crackling theomania. Words
flashed their gold leaf,
a self-swallowing

knotwork of new gospel.
Daniel stormed a lions' enclosure
armed with roast chicken –

once bitten, twice bitten,
his mortal star on marijuana,
unlucky in Leo. His horoscope

foresaw this day, the dark
stranger dressed entirely in fire.

XIII

Flame-throwing Seraph,
bull Cherub, the seven
other breeds of angel.

Feathers break down
by shaft, vanes, lateral barbs,
but a whole

wing of modified finger bones,
cockamamie contraptions
no idiot savant,

no periwigged
fiat lux genius with Tourettes
could plain invent...

the comical penguin,
the hooded clitoris...

XIV

A waterfall. On opposite flanks,
two Panamanian golden frogs;
in semaphore or sumo-dance

a froggy leg lifts up, goes down.
Benjamin worked in stationery,
Rachel export sales, their bond

a gradual sticky. Panama frogs
a-courting by uproarious waters,
voiceless, waving, up and down.

Rachel made sultana cake,
Benjamin offered donuts, glazed.
Soon, high-fives in bowling alleys.

Rush of waters. Love breezed in
like Jesus in a kiss-me-quick hat.

XV

Sarah turns lively, goes jumping
jiminy – pickled on pear brandy,
her Highland Fling

astonishes Damascus: arms antlers,
a 4/4 stomp in red dust. She hums
the great 'Ghillie Callum' or inhales

ragweed pollen, her boot-scuffs
a growing tracery, a *mappa mundi*
the honeybees could follow.

With toe – *heel* – toe – *heel*
she drums up earthworms,
a mucky Lazarus.

Jackdaws gather. Tradition lives
by word of hamstring, Achilles tendon.

XVI

Close, these two, their flock
smattering Low Scandale.
In lambing they lost

identical sleep; shearing,
a synchronised clip.
Dreams, the same, the one

embarrassment of bloodstock.
Their dogs, Bill and Floss,
loved them both equally.

Abel is now dead.
Brother Cain was spotted
high in the Himalayas,

elaborating his grief
with many cartwheels.

XVII

Pigs in spring, happy pigs,
une commune de cochons:
Gloucester Old Spot,

Saddleback, rare breeds
élevés en Écosse
the old-fashioned way,

outdoors, on natural feed,
no antibiotics or influx
of El Diablo, no Beelzebub,

nothing metaphysically
modified in these pedigree
porkers, no sir. So –

come to Ballencrieff
and witness, please, our delirious pigs.

XVIII

Jezebel tuned her acoustic,
sighed, away in a wee dwam.
Strings whinged or grew sweet.

This was Brixton, not Babylon.
She put some lippy on,
settled her bustle, strummed,

her song's upsurge
a knuckling down, her stage
a scaffold, a coronation.

The crowd fell or swam
through shocks of adrenalin,
Venus in flames

as Jezebel, Jehovah's daughter,
raised O'Connor's 'Jerusalem'.

XIX

Borders closed, land
withering and occupied,
men became rabbitwise,

dug tunnels to smuggle
food and munitions, vital
zoo animals: nothing above

cow size or high-necked,
drugged in transit. The city
survived on daily shows,

chickenfeed economies:
fox tame, lion thin, a snowy
donkey they painted

with henna zebra stripes,
gone sad, facing its wall.

XX

Balding young Noah
constructed a classic comb-over.
High wind signalled ruin,

impending rain. He amassed
articles on follicle health, applied
pigeon dung paste,

pomades of hippopotamus fat,
black Andalusian foal urine.
The more elusive ingredients

took jungle-time and steel traps,
an array of live bait, his life
regime and rumour.

Markets rose. Bullet-head Noah
floated his beauty empire.

XXI

Gethsemane: a grassy knoll
fringed with prize daffodils.
Special forces

interrogated molehills,
dusted breadcrumbs, entertained
appleseed possibilities.

Mary gathered soil samples,
odd bits of mown flesh
to reconstruct a mugshot, a man's

pith and pip. At dusk, children
followed a loop of new law,
ran rings around roses, roses –

a scrambled air command, a sole
surviving god, his wow and flutter.

NOTES

Acts (13)

A found poem containing modified extracts from the Song of Solomon and United Nations report E/CN.4/2006/120 entitled *Situation of detainees at Guantánamo Bay* (Leila Zerrougui et al), dated 15 February 2006.

Foxes (16)

The last line is an adaptation of the final line of Robert Nye's poem 'The Frogs'.

Inexpressible Island (26)

The full story of Campbell, Levick, Priestley, Abbot, Browning and Dickason can be found in *The Longest Winter: Scott's Other Heroes* by Meredith Hooper (John Murray, 2010).

The Find (30–31)

This poem relates to the baby mammoth named Lyuba, and is based on an article about her discovery in *National Geographic*, May 2009.

Natural History (37–43)

These poems are a mixture of found material from Philemon Holland's 1601 translation of Pliny the Elder's *Natural History* and original material in the same spirit, including made-up words. I am indebted to James Eason at the University of Chicago for making the Holland translation available online. *Of Mice and Rats* is for my sister Margaret and in memory of Poppy and Willow.